AWAKENING

GAZAN AWAKENING

Ahmed Paul Keeler

EQUILIBRA

EQUILIBRA PRESS

GAZAN AWAKENING

ISBN: 978-1-9161738-2-8

Equilibra Press
Cambridge
United Kingdom

Enquiries: www.equilibrapress.com

CONTENTS

PREFACE

The last months have witnessed the greatest teach-in since the 1960s and the Vietnam War. Zionism, Palestine and the State of Israel have all been studied from every angle. The voices of the traditional Jews, who have condemned Zionism from the beginning, are now being heard. Those Israeli historians who have seen through the Zionist indoctrination have exposed the false Zionist version of history that has mesmerised the West. The hundred-year suffering and persecution of the Palestinians is now fully revealed. I have gathered together my responses to this terrible drama as it has unfolded and offer them to the reader as an attempt at understanding the genocide we are witnessing.

1

ZIONISM'S GREAT DISRUPTIONS

Zionism's Great Disruptions

To understand the nature of the crisis, we have to start at the beginning with the formation of Zionism, and then follow the trajectory of ten great disruptions, which unfolded as Zionism engaged with the world.

However, the story of Zionism's Great Disruptions begins with another kind of Zionism.

Christian Zionism

Christian Zionism appeared in England in the latter part of the 17th century amongst certain Protestant sects. Their core belief was that the Jews had to return to the Promised Land, before the second coming of Jesus Christ could take place.

By the mid-19th century, Christian Zionism had become fashionable amongst influential members of the British aristocracy, including several Prime Ministers, and would go on to play an important role in the British government's support for a Jewish state in Palestine.

Jewish Zionism

Jewish Zionism, however, emerged out of the cauldron of ideas and ideologies that surfaced during the 19th century. It was a time when European philosophers were busy attempting to categorize humanity in terms of race and ethnicity, and the world was being defined by nation states.
The father of Zionism, Theodor Herzl, was a secular Jew, who had turned his back on his religion. The traditional Jew lived by the Torah and was defined by the religion. Herzl recast the Jews as a race and ethnic group.

In his manifesto *The Jewish State*, published in 1896, he describes how the Jewish State could be placed anywhere; his choice was between

Argentina and Palestine. He decided on Palestine, as he felt that this would attract some religious Jews to his cause. However, with the choice of Palestine, another kind of Zionism came into being, which had a very different vision from that of Herzl's; the religious Zionists, by laying claim to the Promised Land, wanted to fulfil the work of the Messiah.

Antisemitism

But what was the magnet which drew Jews to Herzl's cause? It was antisemitism; the Jews in Christendom had suffered centuries of persecution and pogroms. The Jewish state would be a sanctuary where the Jew would be able to live in peace, bringing the benefits of the modern world to its neighbours, and existing like any other European modern state.

The Balfour Declaration

In 1917, the British government, in what both Jewish and Christian Zionists imagined to be a marriage made in heaven, provided the Zionists with the Balfour Declaration, which gave legitimacy to the establishment of a Jewish State in Palestine. For Great Britain, this would provide an enclave in the heart of the Middle East, where they could protect the Suez Canal and the route to India and the East.

From this declaration of support would unfold the series of disruptions leading to the global crisis we are now facing.

First Disruption: Western Jewry

However, the first great rupture had already taken place within Western Jewry itself. Religious Jews believed that their return to the Holy Land as a people could only happen with the coming of the Messiah. For Jews to create a modern state in the Holy Land was an abomination and Zionism was condemned by the Rabbis.

Second Disruption: Western Christianity

Christian Zionism was also declared heretical by all the main branches of Christianity. But after the Second World War it would become a major force in America's support for the state of Israel. With the Holocaust, guilt and pity led to many Christian churches over-riding their theological objections. The issue now divides the Church.

Third Disruption: Palestine

The land of Palestine was a part of the Ottoman Empire and, with Jerusalem at its heart, an important focal point for the three Abrahamic religions.

It was a beautiful land with fertile valleys, mountains, deserts, rivers, and a coastline onto the Mediterranean Sea. The Palestinians were farmers, fishermen, craftsmen, merchants, administrators and scholars; Bedouins with their flocks inhabited the deserts; they were Muslims, Christians and Jews.

The Palestinians were an ancient people, who were joined together through their deep attachment to the land, and their sharing of the Arabic language and culture. In Jerusalem they took care of the holy sites of the three religions, and were hosts to the pilgrims who came from all over the world.

The imposition of the State of Israel upon their land has meant the destruction of Palestine and its people. The Zionist occupation has resulted in a hundred years of conflict, oppression and suffering without end.

Even the land itself is being destroyed. A traditional, sustainable way of life is being replaced by intense modern systems of agriculture and industry, which are leading to water depletion, poisoning of the soil, and polluting of the air.

Fourth Disruption: The Arab World

The violent establishment of the state of Israel impacted the newly-formed Arab states, as the Palestinian population was evicted from its homeland, thus destabilizing the area. This has resulted in seventy-five years of instability, conflict and devastating wars.

Fifth Disruption: Arab Jewry

Arab Jewry did not share the narrative of persecution of the Jews under Christendom. The Arab Jews were fully integrated into the social fabric of their local Arab communities, whilst maintaining their religious practice and identity. With the establishment of the Zionist State, war broke out, and the Arab Jews found themselves caught in the crossfire.

Reluctantly torn from their homes, they were settled in the new state, formed by European Jews who viewed their Arab brethren as inferior. This meant them having to shed their Arab identity, and as a unique culture they have largely ceased to exist.

Sixth Disruption: The Muslim World

Jerusalem is the third holiest city in Islam. As the religious Zionists took over the helm of the Zionist project, their intention to take over all of Palestine, 'from the river to the sea', became clear. Their ambition to erect the third temple on the sacred precinct also became known. In the Palestinian resistance this awoke a religious fervour in what had largely been a secular political cause, and became a concern for all Muslims.

Seventh Disruption: The Zionists Themselves

Zionists are trapped in a false narrative. Their story relates how Palestine was a 'land without people for a people without a land', and how the Zionists found a wilderness, and how they 'made the desert bloom'. There were no 'Palestinians', these were just wandering Arabs who could be at home in any Arab country. The Zionists state that Arabs have always hated the Jews and want to destroy Israel; that Israel has continually sought peace with the Arabs, but to no avail. Instead, they claim their very existence is threatened by terrorism. For the religious Zionist the story is simple: Palestine, together with parts of Lebanon, Syria and Egypt is the Promised Land, and the Jews, as the rightful owners, are fulfilling their destiny.

As we have seen, Zionists have a problem. From the beginning the orthodox Rabbis have condemned Zionism and its messianic claims.

As Zionism flourished and its support in the West was consolidated, the Zionists marginalized the orthodox jews by renaming them ultra-orthodox, in other words 'our lunatic fringe'.

But the tide is turning, and critiques of Zionism are on the rise. Prominent Jewish historians and scholars are revealing the truth of what has taken place, and young Jews brought up in the Zionist cult are now seeing through the narrative. Palestinians and the traditional orthodox Jews are relating their own narratives, and the Zionist narrative is beginning to fall apart. In an attempt to silence any opposition to their policies, they are trying to convince Western governments to pass laws that equate anti-Zionism with antisemitism.

The disruption to the lives of those belonging to the Zionist cult is incalculable. Far from being a safe haven, the State of Israel has been a place of continuous strife and discord since its birth.

Eighth Disruption: Christian Zionists

Christian Zionists are also trapped in a false narrative, and their followers are imprisoned in an ideology that is causing tremendous suffering and perpetuating a terrible injustice. However, a revolt is taking place amongst many young members of this cult, as they also see through the narrative.

Ninth Disruption: The West

The Zionist state could not have come into being, or have been sustained, without three things: the support of Great Britain, the catalyst of the Holocaust that took place in Germany, and the power of America after WWII. Great Britain was the mid-wife that laid the foundations, the Holocaust ensured that the Zionist state would enjoy a protected status, and America has imposed that protected status upon the world.

The deeply engrained antisemitism of Europe and the West culminated in a horror of such evil and inhumanity, that antisemitism was transformed into the cardinal sin, and support for a Jewish State became an article of faith, an act of atonement for the Holocaust. Israel was a special case, to be defended by the West at all cost, and the Arabs, who opposed this new colony in their midst, were the enemy. The Palestinians were either invisible or terrorists. With the establishment of the state of Israel, Zionism spread throughout the West, and became embedded in the Western mindset. Books, films and journalism depicted the Israelis as the heroes and the Arabs as the villains, in the unfolding tragedy of the Middle East.

However, the West's vision of Zionism and the State of Israel has little to do with reality, and this loss of a true perspective is now threatening a global crisis.

Tenth Disruption: Global Disruption

The secular Zionists were responsible for establishing the State of Israel, however, by the 1970s the religious Zionists were at the helm. They never had any intention of allowing a Palestinian state. Their mandate announced that the State of Israel existed from 'the river to the sea'. They are now in the final process of completing their Zionist Project; the West Bank has more than half a million armed settlers in fortified settlements who are busy, with the support of the army, terrorizing and evicting the Palestinians; Gaza is being completely destroyed with the aim of making it uninhabitable, forcing the Palestinians into the Sinai Desert; and al-Aqsa, the sacred precinct, is being controlled by the Israeli army for the increasing use of Israeli Jews, and for the preparation of the building of the temple.

The world is now divided. Those nations that were colonized or suffered under the Western empires can see quite clearly the ethnic cleansing and genocide taking place, but the Western governments remain under the spell of the Zionist illusion. We are being warned that the unremitting slaughter in Gaza, being witnessed by the world, could spiral into a regional or even a global conflict.

2

TERROR FROM THE SKY

The Slaying of the Innocents

The slaying of the innocents by King Herod is a narrative that has depicted for Christians a crime of supreme horror.

The Magi had told King Herod that a child destined to become King of the Jews had been born in Bethlehem. King Herod told the Magi when they found the child to return to Jerusalem and inform him so that he could join them in worshipping him. The Magi were led to the presence of the child Jesus, and in a dream were warned not to return to King Herod.

The narrative continues in the Gospel of St Matthew:

Then Herod, when he saw that he was mocked of the wise men, was exceedingly wroth, and sent forth, and slew all the children that were in Bethlehem, and in all the coasts thereof, from two years old and under, according to the time which he had diligently inquired of the wise men.

The slaying of the innocents has been vividly brought to life by European painters, who depicted the horror as little children were torn from their mothers and butchered by the soldiers.

Guernica

On Monday the 26th April 1937 the Basque town of Guernica was bombed. Guernica was a Republican stronghold, and General Franco had engaged the German Luftwaffe to undertake the mission. Monday was market day. Most of the men were away fighting. In a two hour raid the centre of the town, including the market square, was destroyed. Hundreds of civilians were killed, others were caught under the rubble dying slowly, many were injured and many were maimed for life.

The bombing of the town of Guernica ushered in a new form of industrialized killing. The full horror of the event was brilliantly captured by the artist Pablo Picasso. The lamentation of the mother holding her dead baby, the severed limbs, and the animal parts scattered about sear our imaginations. When the painting was unveiled at the 1937 Paris International Exposition it horrified the world.

This painting followed the tradition of the slaying of the innocents, with one chilling difference; there were no soldiers present, just total chaos, destruction and death that descended from the sky.

WWII

As WWII began and it became clear that Germany would unleash its blitz upon London, the idea that children would be caught up in the bombing was too terrible to contemplate. The docks and factories in East London were seen as the prime targets for the Luftwaffe, and 800,000 children in their vicinity were evacuated to the countryside, so that they were protected from the carnage that would follow.

The war ended with the merciless carpet bombing of German cities and the total destruction of Hiroshima and Nagasaki.

During the Vietnam War, the term 'collateral damage' was introduced, to justify the killing of civilians.

Gaza

One of the last acts in managing an indigenous people who are being replaced by a settler colony is to pen them up in a reservation or concentration camp. Once imprisoned within secure boundaries, they are left to look after themselves, whilst their gaolers control the exit and entry points and what goes in and out of the reservation. This has been the state of Gaza since 2007. However, the Palestinians continued to resist the illegal occupation of what remained of their land.

In an attempt to crush the continuing resistance of the Palestinians, the Israelis instituted a programme of periodic devastation upon the Gazan population, with bombing raids that killed thousands and injured and maimed many more thousands. These bombing raids were called by the

Israelis 'mowing the grass'. They realized they were not able to extinguish the resistance, but these periodic demonstrations of terror from the sky kept things quiet for a time, whilst the Gazans recovered and rebuilt their infrastructure.

The 7th October marked, for the Israelis, the beginning of the final stage of dealing with the problem of the Gazans. As I write, it is day 155 of the genocide that has been unleashed upon Gaza. I need not attempt to describe what has taken place. We have all been the spectators of what has happened. Every atrocity has been meticulously recorded.

The suffering of the children is beyond words.

3

THE POWER OF NARRATIVES

The Israeli Narrative

There are several parts that make up the narrative that Israeli children are taught from an early age. They are told about the pioneers who came to a land without people for a people without a land, and how they entered a wasteland and made the desert bloom. How the Arabs have always hated the Jews and since the founding of the State of Israel have gone to war against them to drive them into the sea, and how the heroes of the Israeli Defence Force have driven back the invaders. That there is no such thing as a Palestinian people, just wandering Arabs that can be at home in any Arab country. And then there is the religious narrative that relates how Israel is the land promised by

God to the Jews, and with their returning to their homeland, they are ushering in the coming of the Messiah.

Finally, there is the Holocaust. The supreme horror of the attempt to extinguish their people is imprinted on their young imaginations, and they are taught that they must be ever vigilant lest it happen again.

Israel has become a fortress with a high wall sealing the Israelis off from a threatening world beyond. The growing child has no contact with Palestinians either within the fortress or in the lands occupied since the 1967 war, until as a young man or woman he or she joins the IDF, and is engaged in policing the Palestinian territories.

On the 7th October Fortress Israel was breached by Hamas. Before this happened the secular and religious Zionists were descending into civil war. The horror of the breach traumatized the nation, and brought them together to combat the enemy. This enemy was evil incarnate, worse than ISIS, worse even than the Nazis. If they were not totally destroyed, having dealt with the Israelis, they would threaten the Jews everywhere. They were a murderous cult that existed only to kill Jews. They were animals. The story of Amalek was invoked, their entire world was evil, men, women, children, their animals and their homes and their farms and orchards, all must be destroyed. In a frenzy of killing the IDF set about its task, cheered on by the citizens of Israel.

The Palestinian Narrative

The Palestinian Narrative differs little from the other narratives of devastation visited upon the many indigenous worlds occupied by European settler colonies, except in one important aspect: Palestine is alone in Africa and Eurasia not to have been able to expel its settler colonists. Vietnam, Indonesia, Kenya, Senegal and many other colonized territories fought bitter wars and were victorious. Algeria was invaded by the French who for more than a hundred years claimed the country as a French province. They settled a million French citizens who took the best land and turned the Algerians into an underclass, forcing them to speak French. But the

Algerians rose up and the French were defeated. The war lasted eight years and cost the lives of a million Algerians.

However, the European colonists were victorious in the Americas and Australia and the indigenous people were either exterminated, or are penned up in reservations or exist as underclasses.

The European settler colonists had to destroy the worlds they were replacing if they were to succeed in their mission. There is nothing more terrible than the destruction of a culture, a society, a humanity. A living organism is torn apart, dismembered, traumatized and destroyed. Its social order, economy, structures, heritage and future terminated. The horrors that indigenous peoples have suffered at the hands of the Europeans and Americans is unimaginable.

The suffering and struggle of the Palestinians continues, for, the settler colony of Israel has been supported by the most powerful forces on earth. First the British and then the Americans; and now, Germany is attempting to atone for its guilt for the Holocaust with its total support of Israel's attempt to finally eradicate the Palestinians and realize their vision of greater Israel, 'from the river to the sea'.

The Western Narrative

The Western narrative has followed the usual trajectory of European settler colonization, with the addition of certain sub- narratives that specifically relate to the Zionist State. The Balfour Declaration was supported by British politicians who were Christian Zionists, believing that the Jews had to return to the Holy Land for the Second coming of Jesus Christ to take place. The Holocaust made a homeland for the Jews a just cause that could not be questioned. However, in essence the State of Israel remains just another European Settler State.

The European Settler narrative passes through three stages. The first stage is the conquest of the indigenous people on the basis that the conqueror is bringing civilization to a savage or backward world. This was clearly enunciated by Churchill in reference to the Palestinians:

I do not agree that the dog in a manger has the final right to the manger even though he may have lain there for a very long time. I do not admit that right. I do not admit for instance, that a great wrong has been done to the Red Indians of America or the black people of Australia. I do not admit that a wrong has been done to these people by the fact that a stronger race, a higher-grade race, a more worldly-wise race to put it that way, has come in and taken their place.

In the second phase, the Settler Colony claims legal ownership, and any opposition by the indigenous people is called terrorism. The great warrior Sitting Bull, Chief of the

Dakota tribes, said to his conquerors, "When you win a battle, you call it a victory, when we win, you call it a massacre".

The final stage is that the indigenous people are either evicted from the territory, become an underclass in the society, or die. The Palestinians are now experiencing the full force of this final phase.

Palestine was conquered by the British who then nurtured the Zionist state, protecting its development. The Americans then forced, through the newly-formed United Nations, its legal status. Western governments can remain with their Settler Colony narrative and believe terrorists are threatening the existence of Israel; however, the rest of the world can see clearly what is actually happening.

4

EDWIN MONTAGU'S WARNING

Zionism in search of a Protector

From its inception in the late 19th century, Zionism was in search of a powerful protector under whose wing it could establish the Jewish state in Palestine. The Zionists' first port of call was the Ottoman Sultan, Abdul Hamid II, who gave them short shrift when they offered to purchase the territory. There followed visits to the great powers, Germany, Russia and France, but to no avail. It was the outbreak of war in 1914 that gave them their opportunity, and it was the British government that would become the protector and enabler for the realization of their project.

The Jewish Cousins

Sir Herbert Samuel and Edwin Montagu were Jewish cousins who both served in the British government during the First World War. One was a Zionist and the other an Antizionist. Sir Herbert Samuel played a leading role in the formulation of the Balfour Declaration, which placed Great Britain firmly behind the establishment of the Zionist state in Palestine. Edwin Montagu vehemently opposed the Declaration.

Edwin Montagu's Memorandum

Edwin Montagu's Memorandum is a lucid response by an orthodox, mainstream Jew who viewed Zionism as a dangerous political creed.

He believed in a fundamental doctrine of traditional Judaism: namely, that the Jews could only return to Jerusalem with the coming of the Messiah. He states with dry humour,

"I have never heard it suggested, even by their most fervent admirers, that either Mr. Balfour or Lord Rothschild would prove to be the Messiah."

Montagu asserted *"that there is not a Jewish nation… It is no more true to say that a Jewish Englishman and a Jewish Moor are of the same nation than it is to say that a Christian Englishman and a Christian Frenchman are of the same nation."* He followed the orthodox doctrine that Jews are defined by Judaism. What binds the Jews is, quote: "*the fact that they profess to a greater or less degree the same religion."*

He challenged the Zionist claim to Palestine. "*I deny that Palestine is to-day associated with the Jews... It is quite true that Palestine plays a large part in Jewish history, but so it does in modern Mahommedan history, and, after the time of the Jews, surely it plays a larger part than any other country in Christian history."*

He could see quite clearly the ethnic cleansing that would take place if the Zionist project was allowed to go ahead and found it incredible that his government should give it the green light. *"It seems to be inconceivable that Zionism should be officially recognized by the British Government, and that Mr. Balfour should be authorized to say that Palestine was to be reconstituted as the "national home of the Jewish people". I do not know what this involves, but I assume that it means that Mahommedans and Christians are to make way for the Jews... When the Jews are told that Palestine is their national home... you will find a population in Palestine driving out its present inhabitants, taking all the best in the country."*

But what exercised Montagu most was what he perceived to be the antisemitic consequences of the establishment of the Zionist state. This was clearly stated in his opening paragraph: *"I wish to place on record my view that the policy of His Majesty's Government is anti-Semitic and in result will prove a rallying ground for anti-Semites in every country in the world."*

The British government did not heed Edwin Montagu's warning.

The Settler Zionist State

After the First World War, with the fall of the Ottomans, the British government was mandated by the newly-formed League of Nations to oversee Palestine. The Balfour Declaration was incorporated into the Mandate, and Sir Herbert Samuel became the first High Commissioner. Montagu's worst fears began to be realized; the ethnic cleansing of the indigenous people began and, after more than a hundred years, is still taking place.

The Palestinians have suffered the full force of the three stages of the establishment of a settler colony; firstly their conquest by a colony supported and armed by the British, Americans and many Western nations; then, the legalization of the colony as a state, when, after WWII the Americans forced, through the newly-formed United Nations, the partition of Palestine, gifting the greater part of Palestine to the new state of Israel, and finally, the third stage, when the Palestinians who resisted this manifest injustice were designated terrorists in their own land.

7th October

What happened on 7th October 2023 was preceded by 17 years of persecution meted out to the Gazans by the IDF. Four times they had 'mown the grass', killing thousands and maiming many more thousands, mostly women and children. Peaceful demonstrations were met with sniper fire, killing and maiming many hundreds. Meanwhile Israeli settlers were illegally occupying the West Bank and East Jerusalem, with Palestinians being ethnically cleansed, and many being murdered by the soldiers supporting the settlers.

And the West did nothing. No reaction. No outrage at the crimes against humanity being committed in plain view. Silence.

The British Government in Denial

When, on 7th October Hamas launched its raid, killing a number of Israeli soldiers, massacring several hundred civilians and taking hostages back into Gaza, Israel was traumatized. Its iron-clad security had been breached. Humiliation and revenge produced an immediate response. The world must know that this was the greatest crime committed against the Jews since the Holocaust. It came out of a blue sky and was an act of pure savagery. Then came the stories from the Israeli PR machine: 40 babies beheaded; mass rapes of women and children; ten children tied together tortured, burned and

executed; women having their babies torn out of their bellies and stabbed to death; babies placed in ovens.
The British prime minister and the leader of the loyal opposition, closely followed by the Archbishop of Canterbury, joined the procession of world leaders arriving in Tel Aviv to commiserate with the Israeli government and its people, and pledge their undying support. The mantra began, 'Israel must be allowed to defend itself'. The bell was rung for the final settler colonial act to begin: the ethnic cleansing and genocide of the Gazans.

The stories that came out of the lurid imagination of the Israeli PR machine should have been sufficient to warn the British government to act cautiously. But it received and propagated whatever the Israelis fed them. Israel was an ally and friend, so the Palestinians continued to be whatever the Israelis said they were.

As I write it is now Day 173 of the annihilation of Gaza. We are witnessing the complete eradication of a world. This is what genocide looks like. All the world is witnessing the total destruction of a people, their history and their entire environment. There is no hiding from the truth. The leaders are announcing publicly exactly what they are doing.

Successive British governments since the Balfour Declaration have been joined at the hip with Israel and have been complicit in the process required to establish a settler colony. One would have expected there to be an awakening to the reality of what is now happening. But both our government and the opposition are embedded in the Israeli narrative, and in a state of denial regarding what is actually taking place. This has led to two disgraceful episodes.

South Africa brought to the International Court of Justice the accusation of genocide against Israel. The court carefully examined the case and decided it had merit, and Israel is now being investigated. The day after the court's announcement, when all attention should have been on this momentous event, the Israeli PR machine lobbed into the arena an accusation against UNRWA that a dozen of its operatives were engaged with Hamas on 7th October. Following the Americans, the British government swallowed the bait and cancelled its funding to the UN body responsible for delivering and distributing aid to Gaza, thus further endangering the lives of the Gazans.

The second disgraceful episode is the attempt to demonize the marches calling for a ceasefire. While the genocide continues and the suffering of the Gazans increases, and the British government continues to arm Israel, the government along with the opposition turns its focus on introducing legislation to criminalize those peacefully demonstrating against the carnage.

Antisemitism

Edwin Montagu recognized the problem that antisemitism posed, but he believed that far from solving the problem, the creation of a Zionist state in Palestine would lead to "*a rallying ground for anti-Semites in every country in the world.*" He argued that if the Jews had their own state, the pressure for them to leave countries in which they were already unpopular and where they would now be viewed as foreigners, would become overwhelming.

However, he could not have imagined the Holocaust and its impact on the establishment of the Zionist state. Antisemitism was outlawed in every Western country, and blind support was given to the Zionist state as a safe haven for the Jews, who would now come under the absolute protection of the West.

Montagu knew little about Arab Jewry, which did not share the Western narrative of persecution. A great tragedy unfolded as Zionism exported the curse of antisemitism to the Arab world, separating the Jews from their Arab cultures and driving them into the Jewish state.

Montagu would not have been surprised at the growth of Israel into a racist, apartheid state, harbouring a fanatical religious sect bent on genocide in order to prepare the way for the coming of the Messiah.

However, I believe he would have been astonished at the continuing complicity of the British government.

This epic tragedy is now playing out. Israel has proclaimed to the world that to be anti-Israel is to be antisemitic. They have attempted to gather all Jews into their project. The world is horrified by the unfolding of one of the greatest crimes of history. Israel is now isolated and Jews everywhere are suffering an exponential rise in antisemitism.

5

THE AWAKENING

The Awakening

It is now day 300 in the Gaza Genocide. Israel has attempted to seal off what is taking place in Gaza from its own citizens and the world by not allowing foreign journalists into Gaza, and murdering Palestinian journalists and their families. The courage of Palestinian journalists who continue to broadcast is incredible, as they struggle, together with the rest of the Gazans, to protect their families and survive. Most of the Western mainstream media is happy to print what Israel gives them; however, social media and YouTube are another matter.

The last ten months have witnessed the greatest teach-in since the 1960s and the Vietnam War. Zionism, Palestine and the State of Israel have all been studied from every angle. The voices of the traditional Jews, who have condemned Zionism from the beginning, are now being heard. Those Israeli historians who have seen through the Zionist indoctrination have exposed the Zionist's false version of history that has mesmerized the West. The hundred-year suffering and persecution of the Palestinians is now fully revealed.

We are living in the post-colonial age. Post-colonial studies feature in many Western universities, and students are well versed in the horrors inflicted by European colonization on the indigenous peoples of the world. That the Palestinians are suffering the final act of settler colonization is plain to see.

Settler colonialism is no longer acceptable, and the Zionists are having to invent ever more outlandish stories to show that they are not a settler colony. They now claim that Palestine has always been their home, and it is the Arabs who are the invaders. But the true history of Zionism is clear.

Zionism and the idea of a Jewish state was born in the heyday of European settler colonialism. Theador Herzl began formulating his ideas in the 1880s, which were crystallized by 1896 with the publication of *The Jewish State*. These were the two decades during which the European powers gathered in Berlin to carve up Africa between them; during which French Indochina was created, and the USA took over what remained of the Spanish Empire.

The French politician Paul Doumer (1857-1932) perfectly expressed the colonizers' mindset when he sought to justify the French conquest of what became French Indochina:

"Southeast Asia is the ideal colony; it has no end of raw materials and would serve as the perfect outlet for our factories' finished products. Just as Rome civilized the barbarians beyond its borders, we too have a duty to extend French culture and religion to the backward people of the world."

In appealing to Europe for the establishment of the Jewish settler colony in Palestine, Herzl invoked the same justifications, but also revealed that the Zionist state would be entirely dependent upon European patronage:

"We should there (in Palestine) form a portion of a rampart of Europe against Asia, an outpost of civilization as opposed to barbarism. We should as a neutral state remain in contact with all Europe, which would have to guarantee our existence." (The Jewish State)

What we are now witnessing is no different from the horrors that Portugal, Spain, France, Holland, Great Britain, Belgium, Germany, Italy, America, Canada and Australia rained down upon the indigenous peoples they were colonizing; the same concentration camps, mass graves, extra-judicial killings, torture, maiming, starvation, and disease that was employed to break the spirit of the people and destroy their cultures and ways of life.

The Gaza Genocide is the final act in the five-hundred-year European colonization of the world. It is in effect placing a mirror before Europe and the West, and revealing the terrible ugliness of its colonial past. The world that was colonized can see clearly what is happening and so can the International Criminal Court and the International Court of Justice.

6

THE FINAL SETTLER COLONY

Mirror of our Past

As I write this it is now the 350th day of the live streaming of genocide in Gaza. Doctors, surgeons, and aid workers who have been in every kind of war zone and area of natural disaster say they have never experienced anything like it. It is unique in the continuous, unremitting terror from the sky that is being visited upon a defenceless population. Children are being murdered, maimed and orphaned, without pity or remorse. When the slaughter ends, Gaza will join the list of the greatest crimes in history.

How is it that all the world can see what is taking place except the Western governments who are arming and supporting Israel? What is it that blinds them to seeing the genocide that is staring them in the face? I would suggest that it is because, if they accepted the reality of what is happening, they would have to admit that the Zionist state of Israel is a European apartheid settler colony in the final phase of ethnically cleansing the indigenous population.

What makes it so difficult for them to admit that this is taking place is that the Zionist state with its ideology is entirely the creation of the West. It is the West that made possible its establishment in the heart of the Middle East, and has since provided the resources to protect its alien presence there.

The reality of the situation is not lost on the rest of the world, those peoples who have been the victims of European colonization; all the suffering of the past is being brought to the surface, with states lining up behind South Africa to support their case at the International Court of Justice.

The powers that are being used against Gaza are the culmination of ideas and forces that were released half a millennium ago; to understand the full horror of what we are witnessing, we need to examine how these forces came into existence, and see how they came together in the creation of the Zionist state.

Western Christendom

Let us begin our examination in Western Christendom: The primary identity of those living within Roman Catholic Europe some 600 years ago was Christian. The Jews within Europe were outside the law, and subject to persecution. The Muslims were portrayed as the existential enemy, and the Jews were condemned as the killers and deniers of Jesus Christ. Islam was seen as a Christian heresy, and Muhammad, peace and blessings be upon him, was considered a false prophet. Christianity was an exclusive religion; either you were a Christian or you were damned.

The Jews, being the only 'other' in Western Christendom, were blamed when things went wrong; when the harvest failed, or when disease broke out, or when a child went missing. The persecution of the Jews by the Catholic Church was terrible, and this continued after the great schism caused by the Protestant Reformation.

The failure of the Crusades to secure the Holy Land, and the breakup of the unity of Western Christendom with the Reformation, ushered in centuries of internecine warfare, shattering the universal identity of the Christian.

Emergence of the Nation State

The void that ensued was filled with the emergence of the nation state. The primary identity of a person went from being Christian to belonging to a nation state. In Christendom, if you asked a person where they came from, they would answer with the name of their town or village, such as Lisbon or Lavenham. With the creation of the nation state the same question would receive the reply, I am Portuguese or I am English. Whereas it is possible to know and belong to Lisbon or Lavenham, the relationships with Portugal and England are simply imaginary constructs.

The investment of these imaginary constructs with unbridled enthusiasm has produced the most devastating wars in history.

The European Renaissance

The Renaissance also appeared out of the disintegration of Western Christendom. The Classical World, a world that had been dead and buried for a thousand years, was dug up and idealized. Caesar replaced the saint at the apex of society, and a new classical age was inaugurated. The Europeans now took on the exclusive mantle of civilization; Europeans were civilized, the rest of the world was inhabited by savages or members of inferior societies.

However, like the nation state, the idea of being the inheritors of what became known as the Classical World, was another imaginary construct.

But the warriors, full of the spirit of Caesar, were now commanding the most lethal killing machines, and the conquest of the world had begun.

The Conquest of Nature

But another conquest was taking place: the conquest of nature. No longer seeking their knowledge within religion, philosophers turned their attention to the material world. Francis Bacon (d.1626) clearly elucidated their intention to place nature on the rack and force out her secrets. The European capacity to wage war was transformed. With each generation, more deadly ways of killing were devised, and used on the defenceless indigenous peoples in Europe's colonial wars.
Gaza has witnessed new heights in the development of technologies for slaughter.

The Idea of Progress

By the end of the 18th century and the beginning of the 19th century, the Europeans were intoxicated with their success. They were conquering the world and conquering nature. They had freed themselves from the past of superstition and ignorance with a new theory that explained their success: the Theory of Progress; they had reached a new level and were creating paradise on earth.

With supreme arrogance, the colonizers claimed that only *they* could make proper use of the lands they were conquering. Thus, we have the Zionists' chant that they came to a land without a people and that they made the desert bloom.

Just as Marxism was the reaction to the horrors of capitalism, so Zionism was the reaction to the horrors of antisemitism. In both cases the solutions put forward by Marx and Herzl relied upon the Theory of Progress. The Zionists believed that they were not only bringing civilization, but also bringing progress to a barbarous and backward people.

Conclusion

To conclude, the Zionist state of Israel is a European settler colony, which claims that it is the bulwark of civilization against barbarism and that it came to a land that was not tended and made the desert bloom. The state is entirely dependent for its existence on America and Europe, and has access to an unlimited supply of the world's most powerful weaponry in its attempt to subjugate the indigenous population.

This last of the European settler colonies, with all the power of America and Europe behind it, has not succeeded in overcoming the indigenous inhabitants.

The Palestinians are a resourceful and resilient people and they are not going anywhere. It has, however, succeeded in bringing to the surface and exposing the horrors of the European past with its overweening arrogance and unbridled cruelty.

7

AND THE BOMBS KEEP FALLING

And the Bombs Keep Falling

And now
the tears are flowing every day
We watch the children of Gaza
being massacred and mutilated
and the bombs keep falling

We witness the lamentation
of the mother cradling her dead baby
and the bombs keep falling.

We wonder at the dedication
of the doctors and nurses
in their bombed-out hospitals
and the bombs keep falling.

We see the desperation
of the citizens and civil defenders
using their bare hands to rescue
those trapped beneath the rubble
and the bombs keep falling

We listen to the journalists
who continue their reporting
whilst their homes and families
are destroyed
and the bombs keep falling

We are amazed at the teachers
who continue their lessons in tents
as their schools and universities
are reduced to rubble
and the bombs keep falling

We are witnesses to the destruction
of the olive groves and farmland
and the starving of the Gazans
and the bombs keep falling

Even the dead are not spared
with graves dug up
and cemeteries desecrated
and the bombs keep falling

The mosques have been destroyed
but the call to prayer
still rings out across Gaza
as the faithful
lift up their hearts to heaven
amidst the rubble
and the bombs keep falling

Gaza may be destroyed
but the indomitable spirit
of the Gazans will remain
when the bombs stop falling.

Printed in Great Britain
by Amazon

49194920R00057